My Science Notebook

# The Moon

By Martine Podesto

Please visit our web site at **www.garethstevens.com**.
For a free catalog describing Gareth Stevens Publishing's list of high-quality books,
call 1-800-542-2595 (USA) or 1-800-387-3178 (Canada).
Gareth Stevens Publishing's fax: 1-877-542-2596

**Library of Congress Cataloging-in-Publication Data**
Podesto, Martine.
    The Moon/by Martine Podesto.
        p. cm.—(My Science Notebook)
    Includes bibliographical references and index.
    ISBN-10: 0-8368-9215-1 (lib. bdg.)
    ISBN-13: 978-0-8368-9215-4 (lib. bdg.)
    1. Moon—Juvenile literature. I. Title.
  QB582.P63    2008
  523.3—dc22                 2008012380

This North American edition first published in 2009 by
**Gareth Stevens Publishing**
A Weekly Reader® Company
1 Reader's Digest Rd.
Pleasantville, NY 10570-7000 USA

This edition copyright © 2009 by Gareth Stevens, Inc. Original edition copyright © 2007
by QA International. First published in Canada by QA International, Montreal, Quebec.

Gareth Stevens Senior Managing Editor: Lisa M. Herrington
Gareth Stevens Creative Director: Lisa Donovan
Gareth Stevens Senior Designer: Keith Plechaty
Gareth Stevens Associate Editor: Amanda Hudson

**Photo Credits:**
p. 6: European Southern Observatory; p. 9: Public domain; p. 17: NASA; p. 25 t: NASA; c: JPL/
NASA, b: JPL/NASA; p. 29: Alexey Sergeev; p. 38 l and r: NASA; p. 39 b: NASA; p. 45 t and
b: Ministry of Tourism and Parks, New Brunswick; p. 55 b: NASA/NSSDC; p. 67: Christian Roux;
p. 70: NASA; p. 72: NASA; p. 93: NASA.

Every effort has been made to trace the copyright holders for the photos used in this book, and
the publisher apologizes in advance for any unintentional omissions. We would be pleased to
insert the appropriate acknowledgments in any subsequent edition of this publication.

Printed in the United States of America

1 2 3 4 5 6 7 8 9 10 09 08

# My Science Notebook
# The Moon

## by Martine Podesto

Science and Curriculum Consultant:
Debra Voege, M.A., Science Curriculum Resource Teacher

**Gareth Stevens**
Publishing

# Table of Contents

Dear Reader,

Have you ever been curious about a **full Moon** — so bright and round in the starry sky? Is the Moon a star? What does its surface look like? Where does the Moon go during the day? What does the phrase "many **moons** ago" mean? These are just a few of the questions that I've answered in this notebook.

To help you understand my explanations, I've included photos, drawings, and simple diagrams, too. I hope you will find the answers to your questions here. Don't forget, scientists ask themselves new questions every day. That's how they learn and make new discoveries. Always continue to ask yourself questions. Like scientists, you'll be amazed by what you discover about the world around you!

Happy reading!

Professor Brainy

South America

✗

Atacama Desert

## Hello, Max!

A few months ago, my friend and I decided to take a long bicycle trip through the Atacama Desert in South America. We were both very excited about visiting one of the most powerful telescopes in the world, the VLT (Very Large Telescope) in northern Chile. Sometimes we rode at night to reach our destination sooner. I can assure you, Max, that our nighttime rides were not dangerous. Our

VLT (Very Large Telescope)

bicycles, helmets, and clothes were equipped with reflectors. Thanks to those little mirrors that reflect the lights of passing vehicles, we were visible and safe. You are probably asking yourself what my bicycle adventure has to do with your question, right? I'm getting to it! You see, even if the Moon seems like the brightest object in the night sky, it is not a star. A **star** is a **celestial body** that makes its own light and heat, just like the Sun. The Moon produces neither light nor heat. It only reflects the light of the Sun, a little like a giant bicycle reflector floating in the night sky.

Regards,
Professor Brainy

How long would it take to go to
the Moon by bicycle?

Thanks, Professor!
Emma, age 10

Dear Emma,

On some nights the Moon is so huge that
even I believe that I could pedal there
before sunrise!

But as appealing as that idea is, it wouldn't be quite that easy. Let's do a little math:

- The Moon is about 239,227 miles (385,000 kilometers) from Earth.

- We could expect to travel at least 6.2 miles (10 km) an hour by bicycle.

According to my calculations, it would take us about four and a half years to get to the Moon. And that's if we rode without stopping.

Whew! No wonder they invented rockets!

Best regards,
Professor Brainy

Did you know that *Apollo 11*, the first manned mission to the Moon, took about 4 days and 6 hours to get there? That's a lot faster than a bicycle!

Hello!

How did the Moon get its name?

Diane, age 12

Dear Diane,

The word *Moon* comes from the Latin word *luna*, which means "glowing" or "bright." Latin is a very old language. It shaped several other languages spoken today, like French, Italian, and Spanish. Because the Moon is the brightest reflection in the night sky, it comes as no surprise that people long ago named it that way!

Many languages have a word for the Moon that comes from the Latin *luna*. Here is a list of the words for *Moon* in different languages:

## The Moon Around the World

| | |
|---|---|
| French: Lune | Danish: Mane |
| Italian: Luna | Russian: Luna |
| Spanish: Luna | Dutch: Maan |
| Portuguese: Lua | Japanese: Getsu |
| Greek: Selini | Turkish: Ay |
| Polish: Ksiezyc | Catalan: Lluna |
| German: Mond | Finnish: Kuu |
| Arab: Qamar | Hungarian: Hold |

Did you know that the Moon has also inspired names for other things found in nature? For instance, there are moonfish, which are large, round, and silvery. There is also a plant called moonwort, whose tiny, disk-shaped seedpods reflect the moonlight. And that's not all! Look at your hands closely. Do you see the little white semi-circles at the base of your fingernails? We call those "half-moons" because that's what they look like!

Your friend,
Professor Brainy

Dear Professor Brainy,

I'm on vacation with my parents in Japan. Yesterday we visited Space World in Kitakyushu. I saw some Moon rock samples there. My father told me that, thanks to these rocks, astronomers and geologists were able to figure out when and how the Moon was formed. How can they learn that from a single pebble?

Domo arigato
(that means "thank you very much" in Japanese),

Louis, age 11

Flag of Japan

*Kon nee chee wa* (Hello), Louis!

Lucky you! Japan is a marvelous country.

The astronauts brought back almost 900 pounds (408 kilograms) of rocks, sand, and dust from the Moon's surface and crust. Astronomers and geologists studied these materials closely. Do you know what? They found that the rocks looked a lot like Earth rocks! Their research showed that Earth and the Moon are the same age (about 4.5 billion years old) and that together they may once have formed a single **planet.**

According to the most popular **theory**, a celestial body the size of the planet Mars may have crashed with Earth when it was a very young planet. This crash would have broken off a large section of Earth's surface. The debris would have drifted in space. Over time, these pieces would have "glued" back together to form the Moon. I've pasted a picture below that shows this theory.

Moon rocks are safely stored at places like the Lunar Sample Laboratory at the Johnson Space Center in Houston, Texas. This lab holds thousands of rocks for scientists to study.

Moon rocks are also displayed at several museums. You can view some of the rocks at the National Air and Space Museum

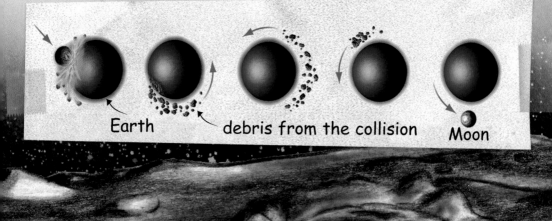

Earth        debris from the collision        Moon

Lunar rock

in Washington, D.C. Moon rocks are also at the Kennedy Space Center in Florida and at the American Museum of Natural History in New York.

*Domo arigato* for your question, Louis!

Professor Brainy

Dear Professor Brainy,

I found this picture in a science magazine. It's an eclipse of the Moon. I find it so amazing! Could you explain what happens during a lunar eclipse? When will I be able to see one?

Thanks!
Joel, age 9

Dear Joel,

A **lunar eclipse** takes place when Earth passes directly between the Moon and the Sun. During a lunar eclipse, Earth blocks the Sun's rays

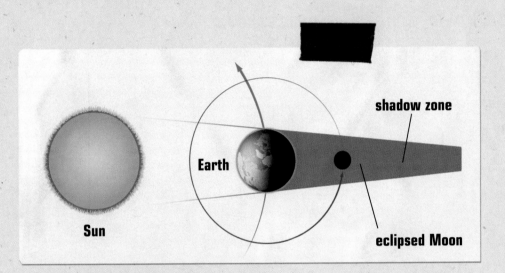

from reaching the Moon. This means our Moon is completely hidden by Earth's shadow. I've added a diagram above to help you understand how this event occurs.

Lunar eclipses are rare, but we can predict the exact time they will take place. Unlike eclipses

of the Sun, which can harm your eyes,
lunar eclipses can be viewed with
the naked eye or with binoculars.
Since the Moon only reflects
the Sun's rays, the light during
a lunar eclipse is not strong
enough to harm your eyes.

So feel free to watch as
closely as you like!


Best regards,
Professor Brainy

Dear Professor Brainy,
Why does the Moon seem to
follow us when we're riding
in a car?

Vicky, age 11

Dear Vicky,

Last summer, I took a train trip across the United States. Through the window, night after night, the Moon seemed to be following me. I found it kind of comforting!

The Moon seems to follow us because it is so far from Earth. Watch the landscape closely on your next car trip. You will notice that the houses, trees, and mountains closest to the car seem to pass by at high speed. The objects that are very far from the road, however, remain visible for a long time — and even seem to follow us for a while.

The farther objects are away from us, Vicky, the more it seems they are moving along with us. Since the Moon is approximately 239,227 miles (385,000 km) away from Earth, it's no surprise that it makes an amazing travel partner!

Have a good trip!

Professor Brainy

Hello, Lawrence,

Not every **planet** has a moon, or a natural satellite. Some planets have none, while others have dozens! Let's take a quick tour around our **solar system**.

Mercury and Venus have no moon. Mars has two. Jupiter has 63; Saturn, 60; Neptune, 13; and Uranus has 27. But wait! By the time you read this, these numbers may have changed. With telescopes becoming more powerful, a new moon may be discovered at any time. When doing research, always check facts in recently published books and on the Internet.

Did you know that other moons in the solar system are very different from ours? Io, one of Jupiter's moons, has volcanoes that "spit" sulfur hundreds of miles into the air. Callisto, another moon of Jupiter, is made of rock and ice and may be hiding a layer of water under its surface. Titan, one of Saturn's satellites, has a thick **atmosphere** similar to the one that surrounded Earth when it was a young planet.

Io

Callisto

Titan

Even though they are very different from one another, moons always have at least two things in common: They orbit a planet, and they only reflect light from the Sun!

Regards,
Professor Brainy

Hello, Professor,

What does the Moon look like?

Steven, age 10

Dear Steven,

Shift your imagination
into high gear! Let's
imagine that we're
traveling to the Moon.
Ready? Three, two, one...
blast off!

Four days and four nights have
passed. We will be arriving shortly. Look
out the window. There is the majestic Moon.
Observe its surface. You will see **craters**,

or deep holes. These craters are the traces of **meteorites** that crashed into the Moon sometime after its birth. Check out the mountain ranges, cracks, and winding grooves that make up the Moon's surface.

We've arrived. Let's climb out. At first sight, the Moon seems like nothing more than rock and dust.

Unlike Earth, there is no trace of life on the Moon. Everything is a shade of gray.

The Moon has no atmosphere, that mixture of gases that surrounds Earth and supports life. Atmosphere also gives Earth its beautiful blue color. On the Moon, the sky always looks black, day and night.

On the Moon, there is no air, no wind, and no sound. As you can see, the Moon is fine for a short visit but not the ideal spot for a long vacation. Shall we head back home?

Best wishes,
Professor Brainy

I read in a book that the dark spots on the Moon are seas. Is that true, Professor? What are the dark spots we see on the Moon?

Cynthia, age 9

Dear Cynthia,

Have you ever heard of the Dead Sea?

The Dead Sea is a very special body of water in Israel. It is so salty that no fish can live in its waters (although some bacteria can). The Dead Sea is really a lake! It was misnamed by one of its discoverers.

The Dead Sea

There are many things and places that have been misnamed: the white rhinoceros (which is not white), the prairie dog (which is not a dog), heartburn (which has nothing to do with the heart but with the stomach) ... and the "seas" on the Moon.

Early astronomers believed the dark spots they observed on the Moon were seas, or lakes, similar to those on Earth. These spots were given elegant names: Sea of Tranquility, Ocean of Storms, Sea of Showers, Lake of Dreams, and Sea of Cold. Even though we now know there is no water on the Moon, we still use these names.

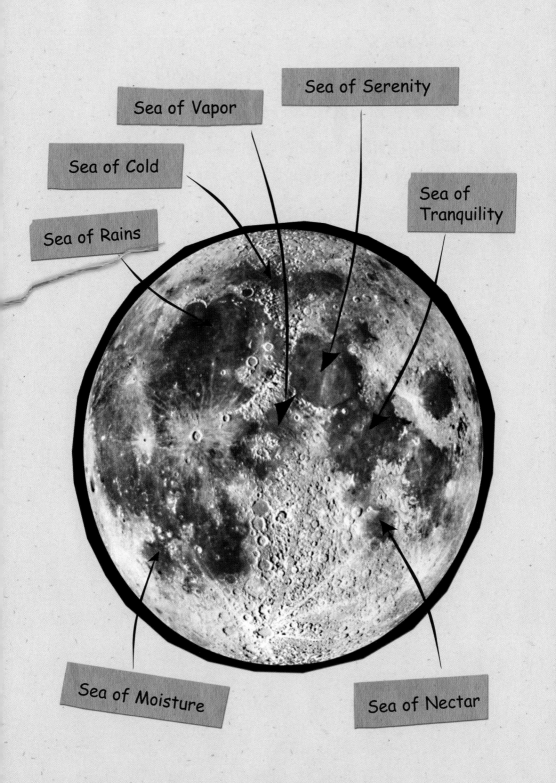

Sea of Serenity

Sea of Vapor

Sea of Cold

Sea of Tranquility

Sea of Rains

Sea of Moisture

Sea of Nectar

The Moon's "seas" are really craters that were formed by the impact of **comets** and meteorites. The craters filled up with hot melted rock that came out of cracks in the Moon's crust, soon after the craters were made. The chemicals in the lava give the **lunar "seas"** their dark color.

Regards,
Professor Brainy

Dear Professor Brainy,

Looking at the Moon last night, I asked myself a question: "Why doesn't the Moon drift away into space?" What I mean is, what keeps the Moon close to Earth?

Megan, age 10

Dear Megan,

More than 300 years ago, an English scientist named Sir Isaac Newton asked himself the very same question. Legend has it that he found the answer to his question when he saw an apple fall from a tree! According to Newton, there is an invisible force that attracts

35

all objects (like apples) to the ground.

Newton believed that this force might also be at work in space. Newton called the force **gravity**. And Newton was right! Gravity does exist in the universe. It is Earth's gravity that keeps the Moon near us.

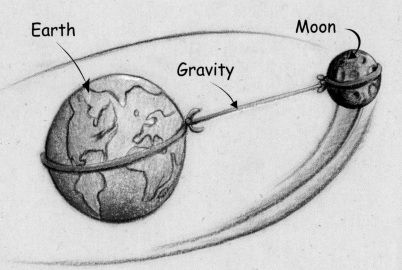

Earth

Moon

Gravity

Here is a simple idea that will help you understand how gravity works.

Imagine that an apple is attached to a string. You spin the apple around you while holding on tightly to the string. It is as if you are the Earth, the apple is the Moon, and the string is gravity. Now imagine letting go of the string. What happens to the apple?

This is what would happen
if there were no gravity:
The Moon would drift away
into space!

Your friend,
Professor Brainy

Dear Professor Brainy,

Who has gone to
the Moon?

Bwarna, age 10

Dear Bwarna,

Americans Neil A. Armstrong and Edwin "Buzz" Aldrin, of *Apollo 11*, were the first humans to set foot on the Moon. Their lunar module was named *Eagle*.

Edwin "Buzz" Aldrin

Neil A. Armstrong

These are the 10 other lucky astronauts who walked on the Moon. I've put the Apollo missions and landing dates below:

- Charles Conrad Jr., commander, and Alan Bean, pilot, *Apollo 12* (November 19, 1969)

- Alan B. Shepard Jr. and Edgar Mitchell, *Apollo 14* (February 5, 1971)

- David R. Scott and James B. Irwin, *Apollo 15* (July 30, 1971)

- John W. Young and Charles M. Duke Jr., *Apollo 16* (April 21, 1972)

- Eugene A. Cernan and Harrison H. Schmitt, *Apollo 17* (December 11, 1972)

No one has returned to the Moon since 1972.

Neil Armstrong's first words as he stepped down onto the Moon will always remain famous:

"That's one small step for a man, one giant leap for mankind."

Regards,
Professor Brainy

Good for you, Lucas!

You noticed that the Moon always shows us its same side. Sorry to disappoint you, but the Moon is never going to show us its other face! This is because the Moon makes a full rotation in 27.3 days — the exact amount of time it takes to revolve around Earth. These movements mean that we always see the same side of the Moon.

This event may be hard to imagine. I suggest you try the following experiment. It may help you understand it better.

Get two Styrofoam balls (they can be the same size). Insert a pencil into one of the balls. Then mark the ball with an "X" on one side. This ball will represent the Moon, and the "X" will be its visible side. Now hold the other ball in front of you. This other ball represents Earth. Take your Moon and make it turn in a circle around Earth, making sure that the "X" is facing Earth at all times. What do you notice?

For the Moon's visible side to remain turned toward Earth, you have to rotate the Moon one complete turn (turning your wrist all the way around to do it!). That is exactly what happens in space.

To see the far side of the Moon, you will have to wait for the day when shuttles transport curious tourists into space!

Your friend,
Professor Brainy

Dear Professor,

I live in New Brunswick, which is in Canada near the Bay of Fundy. We have the highest tides in the world here. These are some photos of the Hopewell Rocks at high tide and at low tide. I'm the one who took the pictures. I know that tides are caused by the Moon (my sister Sarah told me), but I still don't understand how the Moon does it.

Christine, age 9

Dear Christine,

All celestial bodies have gravity. They attract other celestial bodies in space. This force depends, in part, on the distance that separates them. The closer they are, the greater the attraction. The farther apart they are, the lesser the force of attraction. The Moon is the celestial body closest to Earth.

Its gravity can be felt by every object on our planet. That means you, I, your cat, your house — we are all attracted by the Moon when it passes over our heads! Because Earth's gravity is much stronger, however, we barely feel the Moon's pull.

Hopewell Rocks at low tide

It's not the same for the oceans. It is easier for the Moon's gravity to move the ocean than a solid object like a house

Hopewell Rocks at high tide

or a mountain. When the Moon is over the ocean, its gravity pulls the water upward. This pull creates a high **tide**. About six hours later, Earth has made a quarter rotation. The Moon is no longer facing the ocean, so the waters return to normal. This is low tide. Since Earth makes a full rotation in 24 hours, the cycle of tides occurs twice a day (two high tides and two low tides) every day, without end!

The Moon and the Sun are aligned about every two weeks. Then their gravities are combined. This makes them "pull" even harder on the oceans, creating even higher tides. These tides are called spring tides.

Moon

High tide

Earth

Next summer, I plan to take a trip to the Bay of Fundy. It looks beautiful!

Your friend,
Professor Brainy

Dear Professor Brainy,
My little brother Nicholas would like
to know where the Moon goes during
the day.

Melanie, age 12

Dear Melanie,

Thank you for sending me Nicholas's excellent question. The Moon is still there, even if we do not always see it. During the day, the sunlight is so bright that it hides all the other celestial bodies in the sky. At night, the Sun is on the opposite side of Earth. With its rays no longer lighting up the sky, we can see the Moon and the stars. Imagine you held up a bright flashlight and a tiny birthday candle in front of you. With the beam of the flashlight pointed right at your eyes, you couldn't see the tiny amount of light given off by the candle. But if you turned the flashlight so it shined in another direction, the flame of the candle would appear much brighter.

In spite of all this, we can sometimes see the Moon during the day, either shortly after sunrise or shortly before sunset.

Best wishes,
Professor Brainy

Hello, Professor Brainy,

We recently saw a television show about the Apollo missions. Why did the astronauts bounce when they walked on the Moon?

The Martin-Roy Family

Dear Martin-Roy Family,

Gravity is the invisible force that attracts all objects to one another. The larger a celestial body is (which means the more matter it holds), the greater its gravity. Of course, you know that Earth is larger and contains more matter than the Moon. The gravity of our planet is six times stronger than that of the Moon. (This means that Earth "pulls" six times harder on the objects on its surface.) All objects are therefore six times heavier on Earth than on the Moon (or six times lighter on the Moon than on Earth). On the Moon, a six-year-old child who weighs 55 pounds (25 kg) would weigh as little as a three-month-old baby does!

Humans and animals have muscles that are suited for Earth's gravity. In a way, their strength is "fine-tuned" to its exact gravitational force. Where there is six times less gravity, these muscles become much more powerful. That is why the astronauts could make giant leaps with little effort!

Your friend,
Professor Brainy

Dear Professor Brainy,

What do we know about the side of the Moon that we can't see?

Sydney, age 10

Dear Sydney,

Now, there's a question from a truly curious mind! The part of the Moon we cannot see is called its far side. It is the side farther away from Earth.

Probes have been sent into space to explore and photograph it. Thanks to them, we now know that the far side looks a lot like the visible one! One difference is that it has fewer lunar "seas." These are actually lava-filled craters that appear darker than the rest of the Moon's surface. There are fewer of them because the crust is thicker on the far side. Lava moves less easily through thick crust and cannot reach the surface. The Moon's far side also has more craters than the near side. As you can imagine, astronomers have come up with a good theory to explain why the far side has more craters. They think that meteorites have fallen more often on the Moon's far side. Because the far side faces space, it is more exposed to meteorites. Without being able to admire it, you can still imagine what the Moon's far side looks like, with its craters, craters, and more craters!

Visible side

Regards,
Professor Brainy

Far side

In 1959, Soviet space probe *Luna 3* brought back the first photographs of the Moon's far side.

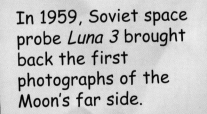

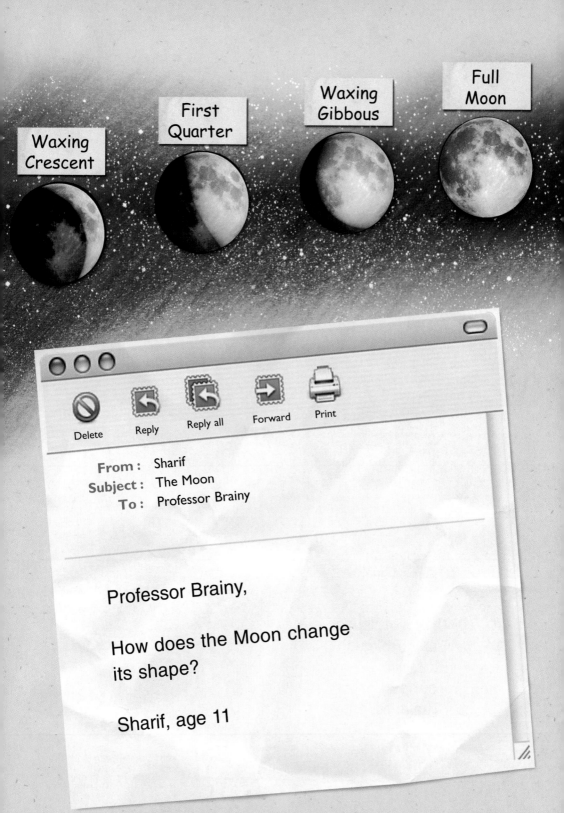

Waxing Crescent

First Quarter

Waxing Gibbous

Full Moon

Delete   Reply   Reply all   Forward   Print

From : Sharif
Subject : The Moon
To : Professor Brainy

Professor Brainy,

How does the Moon change its shape?

Sharif, age 11

Waning Gibbous

Last Quarter

Waning Crescent

New Moon

Dear Sharif,

The Moon's shape does not change. Actually, it is the part of the Moon that is lit up that changes its appearance. Remember, Sharif, that the Moon shines because it reflects light from the Sun. As it revolves around Earth, its lit side looks slightly different every night. The changing Moon "shapes" that you are referring to are called the **phases of the Moon.**

With the help of this illustration, follow the phases of the Moon as it revolves around Earth.

Waning Crescent

Sun

Light from the Sun

New Moon

On the blue circle, we see the Moon's positions in relation to Earth and to the Sun. This blue circle shows the part of the Moon that is being lit by the Sun. On the red circle, we see the phases of the Moon as they are seen from Earth.

Waxing Crescent

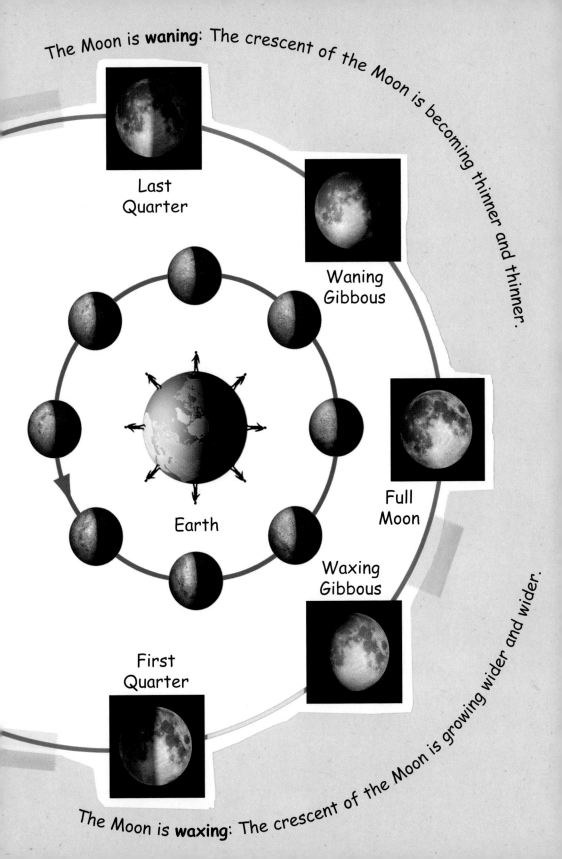

The Moon is **waning**: The crescent of the Moon is becoming thinner and thinner.

Last
Quarter

Waning
Gibbous

Full
Moon

Earth

Waxing
Gibbous

First
Quarter

The Moon is **waxing**: The crescent of the Moon is growing wider and wider.

The first phase is the **New Moon**. The Moon is now between Earth and the Sun. It is not visible because the Sun is lighting up the far side.

In the 14 days that follow, the Moon gradually moves in its orbit around Earth. The crescent grows wider and wider. The part of the Moon that is exposed to the Sun is becoming more and more visible from Earth. The Moon is said to be **waxing**.

Now we get to the phase of the Full Moon. The visible side of the Moon is completely lit up by the Sun. Earth is now between the Moon and the Sun.

During the 14 days that follow the Full Moon, the Moon continues its orbit around Earth. The bright side of the Moon that we can see shrinks, and the crescent becomes thinner and thinner. The Moon is said to be **waning**.

The Moon disappears once more, and another turn around Earth begins!

Yours truly,
Professor Brainy

Dear Mr. Professor,

Is it true that strange things happen during the full Moon?

Yoshi, age 10

Dear Yoshi,

For thousands of years, many people believed that the full Moon had magical powers. The werewolf legend is one of the most famous examples. It is the story of a man who turns into a wolf on nights when the Moon is full.

A number of scientists have done research to find out if the Moon has strange effects. They have studied the behavior of humans, animals, and plants during the full Moon. Do you know what, Yoshi?

Their studies showed that the Moon has no effect on the way people, animals, or plants behave. Magical powers and werewolves are nothing more than legends.

Until the next full Moon,
Professor Brainy

Professor Brainy,
Can you tell me if there is water on the Moon?
Brian, age 10

Hello Brian,

No traces of liquid water have ever been found on the Moon. It seems that there may instead be ice! The presence of ice on the Moon was first suspected in 1996.

The next question you are probably asking yourself is, "How did the ice get there?"

According to scientists, the ice would have arrived with comets that fell on the Moon billions of years ago. A comet is a tiny celestial object. It looks like a ball of snow and rocks mixed together. Crashing into the Moon, the

snow in the
comets would
have turned into
water vapor after
impact. Later, the water
vapor would have cooled
and then frozen, especially
at the Moon's poles. At the
south pole, the ice would sit at the
bottom of craters that are always
cold because they are never exposed to
the Sun. At the north pole, the ice would
be protected by a layer of rock dust that's

about 16 inches (41 centimeters) thick. The Lunar Prospector mission suggests there could be about 13 billion pounds (5.9 billion kg) of ice mixed into the soil at the bottom of the moon's craters!

Take care,
Professor Brainy

Launched in January 1994, American space probe *Clementine* used radar to gather information on the lunar crust. The *Lunar Prospector* probe followed in 1998.

Lunar Prospector

Clementine

Hello Professor Brainy,

What are the patches and spots that we see on the Moon?

Danielle, age 9

Dear Danielle,

I remember the summer when my grandfather and I headed off on an Alaskan adventure. Our hikes sometimes lasted an entire day. At night, we had fun looking at the Moon, seeing imaginary objects in its bright and dark patches. I imagined a dinosaur

Mount McKinley

or a smiling face. My grandfather saw a little man sitting in a tree.

What we actually see
as we gaze at the Moon
are its land features. The
mountains, craters, and lunar
plains form light areas. The "seas"
form dark areas. It is the combination
of the light and dark patches that,
with a little imagination, seems to make
pictures appear!

And how about you,
Danielle? What shapes
have you seen so far?

Your friend,
Professor Brainy

Hello, Maria,

There are three kinds of Moon rocks: basalt (which is dark), anorthosite (which is light), and breccia (which is a mixture of several rocks). These rocks are also found on Earth. On the Moon, however, they have not been worn down by rainwater or oceans. There isn't any water on the Moon!

Basalt

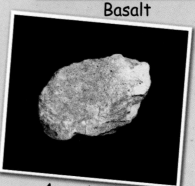

Anorthosite

Breccia

The Moon was probably created after a collision between a large asteroid and Earth. Fragments from the crash would have come together to form the Moon. This would explain why the Moon is partly made up of the same material as Earth. Lunar rocks are not identical to those on Earth, though. This is because the Moon, like Earth, has its own history.

One thing that exists on the Moon but not on Earth is **regolith**. This is a thick layer of dust that covers the Moon's surface. It was produced by the impact of many meteorites. When we look at regolith under a microscope, we see tiny bits of lunar rock. This dust is piled up several inches (centimeters) high.

On July, 20, 1969, U.S. astronaut Neil A. Armstrong left his footprint in the thick layer of regolith on the Moon. Take a look. It is an inch (2.5 cm) deep!

Regards,
Professor Brainy

Neil A. Armstrong's footprint

Hello, Quan-Yung!

Let's take a closer look at the layers of the
Moon. The top layer is the crust, which is
about 43 miles (70 km) deep. The lunar rock
samples brought back to Earth by the Apollo
missions come from the Moon's crust.

Underneath this lies the mantle, a thick layer
about 808 miles (1,300 km) deep. It is made
of rocks that were once very hot but that now
have cooled and solidified.

Finally, the Moon has a core. It measures
about 497 miles (800 km) in diameter.
Researchers think the Moon's core is composed
of iron mixed with other metals. It is not

known if the core is completely solid or a combination of solid and liquid.

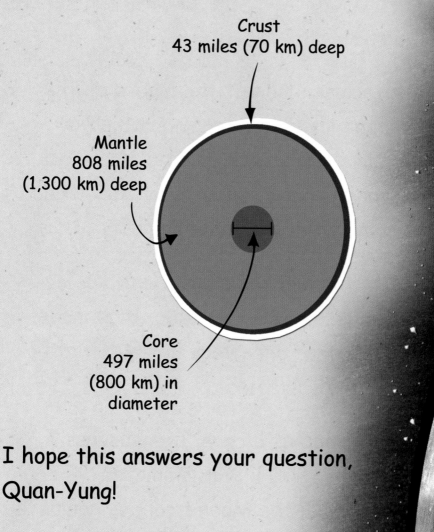

Crust
43 miles (70 km) deep

Mantle
808 miles
(1,300 km) deep

Core
497 miles
(800 km) in
diameter

I hope this answers your question, Quan-Yung!

Best regards,
Professor Brainy

Dear Sebastian,

...y of holes?

Sebastian, age 8

Billions of years ago, the Moon was entirely smooth. Over the years, meteorites crashed into it from every side. Each meteorite left its mark — a large crater here, a small crater there. Some filled up with lava. Others remained empty.

### RECORDS OF THE SOLAR SYSTEM

The largest craters in the solar system are found on the Moon. Giant Aitken, at the south pole, is the biggest. It measures almost 1,400 miles (2,317 km) in diameter and is 7.5 miles (12 km) deep.

A meteorite is a piece of a celestial body that crashes into Earth or another celestial body, such as the Moon.

If the meteorite is large enough, it forms a crater on impact. There are more craters on the Moon than on Earth. This is because the Moon does not have an atmosphere to protect it. As meteorites come into contact with Earth's atmosphere, they are usually destroyed, leaving only a trail of dust. It is possible, however, for a very large meteorite to pass through the atmosphere without breaking up. In this case, it crashes into Earth and forms a crater!

Take care,
Professor Brainy

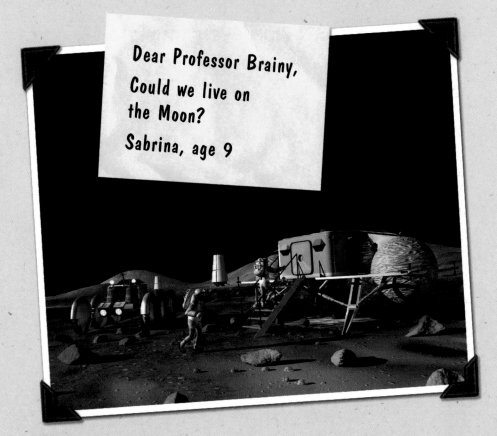

Dear Professor Brainy,
Could we live on
the Moon?
Sabrina, age 9

Dear Sabrina,

Humans need oxygen, food, water, and
temperatures neither too hot nor too cold
in order to live. Unfortunately, none of
these needs can be fulfilled on the Moon.
This makes it impossible for us to live
there ... at least for now!

Someday, scientists and even tourists might stay on lunar bases that have been transformed into little towns. These lunar towns will make it easier for scientists to explore the Moon in more detail and to observe space more clearly.

On Earth, our atmosphere and lights prevent us from seeing into space as clearly as we would like. It would be easier for astronomers to study the universe from the Moon.

Did you know that gravity, the force that attracts objects to the ground, is six times less powerful on the Moon than it is on Earth? This means that we would need less energy and less fuel to launch satellites, telescopes, space probes, and shuttle crews from the Moon. We may one day even go to Mars from there!

Who knows, you may be one of the first people to spend the night at a Moon base, under the stars and with a view of Earth.

Regards,
Professor Brainy

Hi, Professor Brainy!

What would happen if there was no more Moon?

Julio, age 10

Hello, Julio,

I shudder to think of the world without a Moon! Our planet would be very different. Without the Moon, the tides would not be as strong as they are now. Much of our ocean life would suffer. And that's not all. The force of attraction that the Moon has over Earth helps to keep our planet tilted on its axis. Did you know, Julio, that Earth is slightly tipped to one side, a little like a top when it isn't spinning?

Axis

This slight tilt of our planet is also partly responsible for the seasons.

Without the Moon, Earth would be tossed about in space! Our seasons would be different from what they are now. Without the seasons, plants wouldn't bud in the spring each year. Animals would no longer migrate. Lakes would freeze over or evaporate.

So when you look up at the night sky, Julio, remember that the Moon is more than just a pretty face!

Yours truly,
Professor Brainy

Dear Colette,

The Moon is part of many expressions
in our language. In this case, your
teacher is talking about something
that happened a very long time ago.
We find the word *moon* in other
expressions, too. For example, when
your mother says that you clean your
room "once in a blue moon," it means
you almost never do it! And if, one

day, you ask your father for 33 new pairs of sneakers, he will probably say, "You're asking for the moon!" That means you are asking for something that is impossible.

Take care!

Your friend,
Professor Brainy

Dear Professor Brainy,

For a school project, I would like to pretend that I am packing my bags for a trip to the Moon. My problem is that I don't know what clothes to put in my suitcase. Is it hot or cold on the Moon?

Sonia, age 10

Dear Sonia,

My Aunt Sophie used to say, "The key to a successful vacation lies in the packing." I think this would be especially true for a trip to the Moon!

The Moon is a little like the Sahara Desert. It has hot days and cold nights. But the weather on the Moon is even more extreme, because it has no atmosphere like the one that protects us on Earth. On the Moon, it is more than 257° Fahrenheit (125° Celsius) during the day and about -238° F (-150° C) at night.

Don't forget that lunar days and nights are two weeks long! For your trip, I suggest you pack a spacesuit.

A spacesuit keeps astronauts cool when temperatures are too hot, and helps them stay warm when it is very cold. Spacesuits are designed to protect astronauts from the Sun's dangerous radiation. Spacesuits also carry an oxygen supply — a very practical thing to have in space!

Your friend,
Professor Brainy

When astronauts go into space, they wear spacesuits to protect them from heat, cold, and small meteorites. The visor of the helmet is coated with a thin layer of gold that protects the astronauts' eyes from the dangerous rays of the Sun.

Dear Professor,
If we manage to set up a base on the Moon, and we find ice there, could we turn it into mineral water?
Louise, age 10

Dear Louise,

A drink of "Moon water" sounds so refreshing! What do you think it would taste like? I imagine it as clear and pure as our own mountain spring water. It would have to be filtered first, though, because it's actually ice mixed with rocks and dust.

Moon water

Once the ice is melted and purified, it could be used for drinking water. Ice, like water, is made up of oxygen and hydrogen. If these components could be separated, we would have a supply of oxygen for breathing instead of having to transport it to the Moon. (On Earth we breathe the oxygen that's in the air.)

As for the hydrogen, we could use it as rocket fuel. Hydrogen is already used to launch rockets from Earth. It's a little like the gasoline we put in the tank of a car to make it run. So, we would have what we need for drinking, breathing, and filling rocket fuel tanks. We would also have lighting for those long, dark nights on the Moon that last two weeks! Solar power would make lights possible. Scientists have figured out that solar panels could be made out of regolith, or the Moon's surface dust. Solar panels capture sunlight and transform it into electricity. They could be made on the Moon, using materials already found there!

Take care,
Professor Brainy

Hi, Professor Brainy,
Can you tell me what the astronauts did when they went to the Moon?

Enrique, age 11

Dear Enrique,

On any mission, I imagine, the astronauts must have taken a little time to admire our blue planet, with its long white streaks of clouds. Let's take a look at what the astronauts did on their missions.

In July 1969, *Apollo 11*'s Armstrong and Aldrin spent more than two hours on the Moon. They collected nearly 45 pounds (20 kg) of Moon rock and carried out scientific experiments.

In November 1969, the *Apollo 12* astronauts gathered about 65 pounds (29 kg) of Moon rock samples and traveled more than half a mile (1 km). And you will never guess what the *Apollo 14* astronauts did in January 1971: They played golf! You see, Enrique, even fun and games are possible on the Moon! Before the astronauts had their round, however, they managed to pick up about 100 pounds (45 kg) of pebbles.

On the *Apollo 15*, *16*, and *17* missions in 1971 and 1972, the astronauts used all-terrain vehicles for traveling longer distances: 15 miles (24 km) with *Apollo 15* and *16*, and 22 miles (35 km) with *Apollo 17*. This last mission brought back more than 240 pounds (109 kg) of Moon rocks!

But not every astronaut on a mission walked on the Moon. One member of the crew always had to remain inside the command module while the others went off in the lunar module to explore the surface. This crew member was responsible for helping the lunar module get back to the command module after its journey. And what about you, Enrique? If you went to the Moon one day, what would be your favorite pastime? Hiking? A game of tennis? Anyway, you still have a little time to make up your mind before you go!

Best regards,
Professor Brainy

Photo of the all-terrain vehicle on the lunar surface during the *Apollo 17* mission

# ⌒ Glossary ⌒

**atmosphere** the layer of gases surrounding a celestial body, such as Earth; air

**celestial body** a natural object in the sky

**comet** a tiny celestial object made up of ice, dust, and gas, which forms a long tail as it orbits the Sun

**crater** a bowl-shaped hole on the Moon's surface formed by the impact of a meteorite

**full Moon** when the side of the Moon visible to Earth is completely lit up by the Sun

**gravity** the force exerted by a planet, such as Earth, or another celestial body that pulls objects toward its center

# Glossary

**lunar eclipse** an event that occurs when Earth passes between the Moon and the Sun, blocking the Sun's light from reaching the Moon

**lunar "sea"** a crater that was filled up by lava flowing out of cracks in the Moon's crust and that is seen as a dark area on the Moon's surface

**meteorite** a piece of stone or metal that falls from the sky and hits the ground

**moon** a celestial body that orbits a planet; also called a natural satellite

**new Moon** when the Moon is aligned between the Sun and Earth so that the Moon reflects no sunlight toward Earth

# ~ Glossary ~

**phases of the Moon** the changes in the Moon's appearance caused by sunlight reflecting off the Moon as it orbits Earth

**planet** a large celestial body that orbits the Sun or another star

**regolith** the thick layer of dust that covers the Moon's surface

**solar system** the Sun and all the celestial objects that travel around it

**star** a massive ball of gas in the sky that makes its own light and heat

**theory** a general rule offered to explain experiences or facts

# ⌒ Glossary ⌒

**tides** the rise and fall of ocean and inlet waters produced by the gravity of the Moon and Sun

**waning Moon** when the part of the Moon exposed to sunlight is becoming less visible from Earth

**waxing Moon** when the part of the Moon exposed to sunlight is becoming more visible from Earth

# For More Information

**Books:**

*Footprints on the Moon.* Alexandra Siy (Charlesbridge Publishing, 2001)

*Home on the Moon: Living on a Space Frontier.* Marianne Dyson (National Geographic Children's Books, 2003)

*The Man Who Went to the Far Side of the Moon: The Story of Apollo 11 Astronaut Michael Collins.* Bea Uusma Schyffert (Chronicle Books, 2003)

*The Moon.* Seymour Simon (Simon & Schuster, 2003)

*New Atlas of the Moon.* Serge Brunier (Firefly Books, 2006)

*Night Sky Atlas.* (DK Publishing, 2007)

*Team Moon: How 400,000 People Landed Apollo 11 on the Moon.* Catherine Thimmesh (Houghton Mifflin, 2006)

# For More Information

**Web sites:**

**National Aeronautics Space Administration**
www.nasa.gov

**National Geographic: Moon Exploration**
science.nationalgeographic.com/science/space/
space-exploration/moon-exploration-article.
html?nav=A-Z

**Smithsonian Education IdeaLab:**
**Walking on the Moon**
www.smithsonianeducation.org/students/idealabs/
walking_on_the_moon.html

**BBC Science & Nature: Space**
www.bbc.co.uk/science/space

**Publisher's note to educators and parents:** Our editors have carefully reviewed these web sites to ensure that they are suitable for children. Many web sites change frequently, however, and we cannot guarantee that a site's future contents will continue to meet our high standards of quality and educational value. Be advised that children should be closely supervised whenever they access the Internet.

# ~ Index ~

## — ABCDE —

Aldrin (Edwin) 39, 40, 93

Apollo missions 12, 39-41, 51, 75, 93-95

Armstrong (Neil) 39-41, 73, 74, 93

astronaut 12, 17, 39, 40, 51, 53, 73, 88, 89, 93, 94

atmosphere 27, 30, 78, 80, 87, 96

comets 34, 66, 67, 96

craters 28, 34, 55, 56, 67, 68, 70, 77, 78, 88, 96

eclipse of the Moon (lunar eclipse) 20, 21, 22, 96

## — FGHIJ —

far side (of the Moon) 42-45, 54-57, 62

First Quarter (Moon) 61

Full Moon 61, 62, 63, 64, 65, 96

gravitational force or force of gravity (*see* gravity)

gravity 36, 37, 38, 46, 47, 48, 51, 52, 53, 80, 96

ice 27, 66, 67, 68, 90, 91

## — KLMNO —

Last Quarter (Moon) 61

lunar bases 80

lunar modules (*Eagle, Intrepid, Antares, Falcon, Orion, Challenger*) 39, 40, 41, 95

# Index